Goodnight Caseville...

Copyright © 2021 by Amy Marie Moore
All rights reserved. This book or any portion thereof
may not be reproduced or used in any manner whatsoever
without the express written permission of the publisher
except for the use of brief quotations in a book review.
Photos are courtesy of family and friends.

Created in the United States of America
First Printing, January 2021

ISBN 0-978-0-578-83507-5

Sweetwater Bay Books
www.sweetwaterbaybooks.com
sweetwaterbaybooks@gmail.com

For Caseville and all of its people, big and small. The charm of this small town is intoxicating and its pull overwhelming. One can't help but fall in love with it and dream of it.

Caseville is a pretty little town situated on the sandy shores of Saginaw Bay in the 'Thumb' of Michigan. Its natural harbor, located at the mouth of the Pigeon River, draws boating and fishing enthusiasts from all around. Beautiful forests and shade trees wind gracefully through the town, creating a cozy atmosphere.

First settled in the mid-1800s, it has functioned throughout the years as many things; a prosperous lumbering town, a plentiful fishing town, a productive farming town, and now, a thriving tourism town. Some consider it their secret little paradise, with its peaceful and beautiful surroundings winning them over year after year. It is most definitely a place that dreams are made of.

This book is a tribute to the town, its people, its places, and the many things that make it so special. As you read through the pages and say goodnight to some of those things, you may find yourself adding to the list and defining what it is that makes Caseville a special place to you.

Goodnight campers filled with people.

Goodnight farmers and your crops.

Goodnight stars,
I'll make a wish.

Goodnight mini golf, providing great fun year after year.

Goodnight festival, too big for words.

Stay in my dreams
long after I wake.

Let's take a closer look.

THE BEACH ~ Caseville is home to a beautiful and sandy public beach, complete with a picnic area, play ground, kayak, kiteboard and paddleboard rentals, volleyball nets, and even a beachfront restaurant! The water is warm and shallow, making it perfect for kids to play in. Summer days find the beach filled with beach chairs and towels, sun bathers, umbrellas, sandcastles, and an abundance of activity.

THE STEEPLE ~ Towering over all other buildings in town, the steeple of the Methodist Church of Caseville has been known to guide boats to the mouth of the Pigeon River since the 1870s. Standing 70 feet tall, this landmark, located on the north end of Main Street, has also welcomed travelers to the center of town for ages.

THE CAMPERS ~ Every season the area welcomes a multitude of visitors with their campers in tow, anxious to enjoy everything that Caseville has to offer. From swimming, fishing, boating, shopping, enjoying festivals, and spending time with family and friends to roasting marshmallows by the campfire. The Caseville area has several family friendly campsites available for all of those happy campers out there.

THE SUNSETS ~ With its shores facing west, Caseville is known for the colorful and dazzling sunsets that are displayed over the water every evening. Each sunset is uniquely beautiful, and most certainly look like they may have even been sent from heaven.

THE SHOPS ~ Main Street is full of restaurants, gift shops and boutiques. Many venture up to town to grab a bite to eat and stroll through the shops to find that special t-shirt, unique gift or vintage find. For well over a century, entrepreneurs have continued to show their faith in the future of this small town by opening businesses along Main Street.

THE FARMERS ~ Caseville is surrounded by rich farmland, which keeps those farmers busy growing and harvesting crops such as corn, sugar beets, dry beans, wheat, and more. Some of this delicious locally grown produce can even be purchased at the Caseville Market on Main Street, which takes place every Saturday. Farmers, we appreciate all that you do!

SUMMER COTTAGES ~ When the weather begins warming up, the population in and surrounding the small town of Caseville begins to swell. Summer cottages throughout the Sand Point area and along M25 come alive with summer vacationers. They flock to their cottages to relax with family and friends and enjoy the simpler things in life.

THE FISH ~ In the early 1900s, commercial fishing was a big industry for Caseville. Back then, a species of fish called Sturgeon were plentiful and the catch of choice. While the Sturgeon have long since dwindled, Caseville is still known for its sport fishing. On any given day, anglers of all ages can be found on the lake, casting a line for Perch, Walleye, Salmon, Whitefish, and Bass. Even the water tower displays a fish, signifying the popularity of the sport and its history with the town.

THE STARS ~The dark nighttime skies over the wide-open waters of Lake Huron are ideal for stargazing. Look up to see constellations, planets, the moon, twinkling stars and maybe even the Northern Lights. Gaze long enough, and you may even catch sight of a shooting star. Don't forget to make a wish!

FIREWORKS ~ Many may agree that Caseville hosts one of the best 4th of July firework shows around. With the works launched from the breakwall, the spectacular light display they create can be viewed for miles around. People gather at the public beach and along the shores of Saginaw Bay to watch. Many even choose to view the show from their boats out on the water.

THE DEER ~ Quite a few deer families live in the beautiful wooded areas within and surrounding the town of Caseville. They visit the lake in the early mornings and late evenings for a cool drink of fresh water. While out and about, they've been known to eat plants from cottage gardens when no one is looking. Take a slow drive through the Sand Point area at dusk, and you will surely see a deer or two!

MINI GOLF ~ This little gem has been around since the late 1950s. Throughout its history, it has provided families with many delightful memories. In addition to mini golf, this place has entertained visitors with bankshot basketball, bumper boats, a giant slide, a game room, and go-kart racing. You can now even complete your visit with a scoop of hand dipped ice cream!

THE BOATS ~ Having fun on the water is a huge draw for residents and vacationers heading to Caseville. Take a look out into the lake, and you are sure to spot speed boats, ski boats, fishing boats, jet boats, pontoon boats, jet skis, kayaks, canoes, kiteboards, paddleboards, and sailboats busying the waters of Saginaw Bay. This beautiful bay is said to be a boater's dream.

THE BIRDS ~ No matter where you look, you can find a bird of some kind in Caseville. You'll find birds such as Gulls, Herons, Geese, Purple Martins, Egrets, and even Eagles! Some of these feathered friends love Caseville so much that they hunker down and stay for the winter instead of flying south to a warmer climate. I think I may even know a few humans who do the same. ;)

THE FESTIVAL ~ Caseville is home to a handful of festivals, but the 10-day long Cheeseburger Festival is what put this little town on the map! Its days are filled with cheeseburger stands up and down the streets, live tropical music, a colorful parade, vendors galore, and a Parrothead or two. Mr. Buffet himself may even turn up joining in on the festivities one day. It is definitely a must-see festival for your bucket list.

THE BREAKWALL ~ Made of concrete and stone and stretching 1500 feet long, a walk on the Caseville Breakwall is an experience not to be missed. Built at the mouth of the Pigeon River, it allows for safe passage into the harbor. Boats can easily follow the wall's bright green light for up to six miles away, allowing for safe guidance in the dark. Many a traveler has walked it, fished it, photographed it, enjoyed its spectacular views, and leaned against its railing to watch the boats glide in and out of the harbor.

THE LAKE ~ Lake Huron is the second largest of the five Great Lakes. It also forms the eastern outline of Michigan's 'Mitten,' including the distinctive 'Thumb,' which shelters Saginaw Bay. Early explorers called it 'the sweet freshwater sea.' It does appear to be as big as an ocean, and it is pretty sweet, so I think I'll have to agree with them. Many often find themselves staring out at that sweet freshwater sea for hours, as its seemingly neverending beauty is extremely captivating.

CASEVILLE, MICHIGAN ~ A place filled with the things that dreams are made of.

www.ingramcontent.com/pod-product-compliance
Lightning Source LLC
Chambersburg PA
CBHW041157290426

44108CB00003B/97